Accelerated

9

Point value: 5

MAR 05 2013

Life Under the Sea

Walruses

by Cari Meister

Bullfrog Books

Ideas for Parents and Teachers

Bullfrog Books give children practice reading informational text at the earliest levels. Repetition, familiar words, and photo labels support early readers.

Before Reading

- Discuss the cover photo with the class. What does it tell them?
- Look at the picture glossary together. Read and discuss the words.

Read the Book

- "Walk" through the book and look at the photos. Let the child ask questions.
- Read the book to the child, or have him or her read independently.

After Reading

- Prompt the child to think more. Ask: What other animals do you think are the walrus' enemy?

Bullfrog Books are published by Jump!
5357 Penn Avenue South
Minneapolis, MN 55419
www.jumplibrary.com

Library of Congress Cataloging-in-Publication Data
Meister, Cari.
 Walruses / by Cari Meister.
   p. cm. -- (Bullfrog books: life under the sea)
 Summary: "This photo-illustrated nonfiction story for young readers describes the body parts of walruses and how they fight with their tusks. Includes picture glossary"--Provided by publisher.
 Includes bibliographical references and index.
 ISBN 978-1-62031-013-7 (hardcover : alk. paper)
 1. Walrus--Juvenile literature. I. Title.
QL737.P62M45 2013
599.79'9--dc23
                                    2012008434

Series Editor: Rebecca Glaser
Series Designer: Ellen Huber
Production: Chelsey Luther

Photo Credits: Corbis, 6–7, 23tr; Dreamstime.com, 13, 23bl; Getty, 20–21; National Geographic Stock, 12–13; Shutterstock, 1, 3t, 3b, 4, 11, 17, 22, 23tl, 24; Superstock, cover, 5, 8–9, 10, 14–15, 16, 18–19, 23br

Printed in the United States of America at Corporate Graphics in North Mankato, Minnesota
7-2012/ PO 1125
10 9 8 7 6 5 4 3 2 1

Table of Contents

Walruses Under the Sea

A walrus swims.
The water is icy.
But he is not cold.

5

He has thick blubber.
It keeps him warm.

It helps him float.

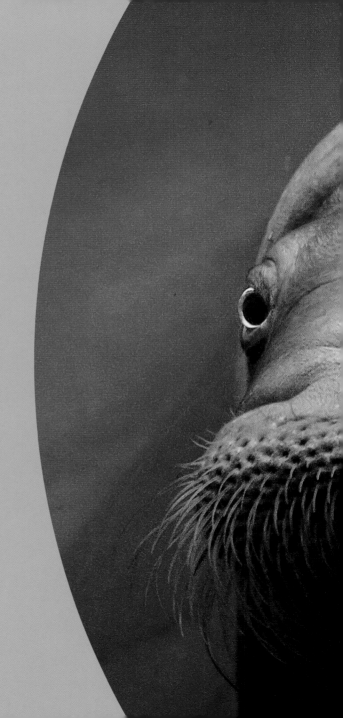

Look at his face.
His nostrils
are closed.

They shut when
he swims.

nostril

whiskers

The walrus has poky whiskers.
They feel for food.

Yum!
A clam!

tusk

What are his long
teeth? They are tusks.

They chop breathing
holes in ice.

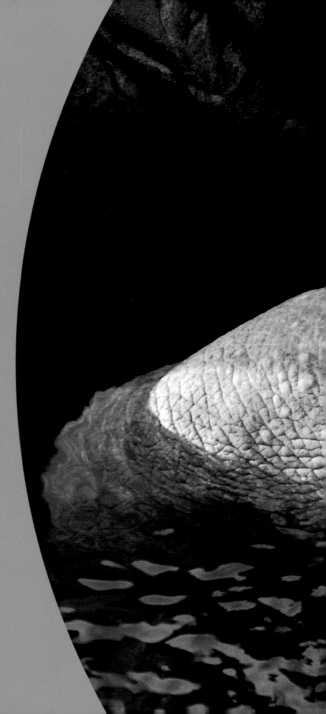

Tusks are
like arms.

They help the
walrus get up.

Tusks are good for fighting.

Look out!
A polar bear!

The bear bites.
He claws.

17

The walrus jabs.
He makes a cut.
The bear
runs away.

The walrus wins!

21

Parts of a Walrus

nostrils
Holes in the nose for breathing.

whiskers
Stiff hairs around a walrus' mouth that help sense things.

tusk
A long, curved, pointed tooth that sticks out of a mouth.

flipper
The front limb of a walrus that helps it swim.

Picture Glossary

blubber
A thick layer of fat under a walrus' skin; it keeps walruses warm in cold water.

float
To rest on water without sinking.

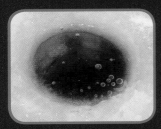

breathing hole
A hole chopped in the ice so a walrus can come to the surface and breathe.

jab
To poke someone with something sharp.

Index

To Learn More

Learning more is as easy as 1, 2, 3.

1) Go to www.factsurfer.com

2) Enter "walrus" into the search box.

3) Click the "Surf" button to see a list of websites.

With factsurfer.com, finding more information is just a click away.